EAGLES

LIVING WILD

LIVING WILD

Published by Creative Education
P.O. Box 227, Mankato, Minnesota 56002
Creative Education is an imprint of The Creative Company
www.thecreativecompany.us

Design and production by Mary Herrmann
Art direction by Rita Marshall
Printed by Corporate Graphics in the United States of America

Photographs by Alamy (Blickwinkel, E. R. Degginger, Nature Picture Library, Andy Rouse-Wildlife, Genevieve Vallee), Corbis (Arthur Morris), Dreamstime (Bateman2000, Bluebuddha, Karoline Cullen, Paul Gibbings, Hkratky, Jomann, Ryszard Laskowski, Mark Martin, Paula Masterson, Mav888, Outdoorsman, Saniphoto, Nico Smit, Gea Strucks, Tormentor, Ling Xia), Getty Images (Drew Hallowell, Klaus Nigge, Adina Tovy), iStockphoto (Bryant Aardema, Anthony Baggett, Mariya Bibikova, Dmitry Deshevykh, Jonathan Heger, Marie Ishikawa, Danish Khan, Manfred Konrad, Jim Kruger, Hans Laubel, Frank Leung, Tommy Martin, Jelena Popic, Spas Popov, Bart Sadowski, Zoran Simin, Lori Skelton, Nico Smit, Jean Van Der Meulen, Terry Wall, Dan Whobrey, Yula Zubritsky), NASA/courtesy of nasaimages.org, Karen Talbot

Library of Congress Cataloging-in-Publication Data
Gish, Melissa.
Eagles / by Melissa Gish.
p. cm. — (Living wild)
Includes bibliographical references and index.
Summary: A look at eagles, including their habitats, physical characteristics such as their keratinous beaks, behaviors, relationships with humans, and admired status in the world today.
ISBN 978-1-58341-968-7
1. Eagles—Juvenile literature. I. Title. II. Series.

QL696.F32G57 2010
598.9'42—dc22   2009025169

CPSIA: 120109 PO1092
First Edition
9 8 7 6 5 4 3 2 1

☙ CREATIVE EDUCATION

EAGLES

Melissa Gish

From atop her perch on one of the tallest trees,
a female bald eagle begins gliding down

toward the lake, her wings outstretched to
about seven feet from tip to tip.

It is early June in the Canadian Rockies, and sunlight shimmers on the smooth surface of Moraine Lake. Tall evergreen trees line the banks of the lake, filling the crisp morning air with the tangy scent of pine. From atop her perch on one of the tallest trees, a female bald eagle begins gliding down toward the lake, her wings outstretched to about seven feet (2 m) from tip to tip. She has spied a swarm of damselflies that have attracted fish, which are popping to the water's surface to catch the insects. Suddenly, the eagle flaps her wings hard and dives toward the water. In one smooth movement, she skims the surface, thrusts her feet downward with a quick splash, and snatches a fish. Then she lifts herself skyward again and circles around, heading back to the treetops, where she will land on a sturdy branch and devour her meal.

WHERE IN THE WORLD THEY LIVE

■ **Bald Eagle**
North America, from Canada to northern Mexico

■ **Golden Eagle**
North America, Europe, North Africa, Asia

■ **Short-toed Eagle**
northern borders of Mediterranean Sea, Russia, Middle East

■ **Steller's Sea Eagle**
Sea of Okhotsk and Russian Kamchatka Peninsula

■ **Bateleur**
Africa and Arabia

■ **Long-crested Eagle**
southern Africa

The 59 eagle species are found on every continent except Antarctica. Categorized by habitat requirements and physical characteristics, the largest group, booted eagles, is also the most widespread, while giant rainforest eagles are the most contained. Sea eagles and serpent eagles make up the other groups. The colored portions of the map represent the habitats of select species from each group.

■ **African Fish Eagle**
Africa

■ **Martial Eagle**
Africa

■ **Tawny Eagle**
Africa, southwestern Asia to India

■ **Philippine Serpent Eagle**
Philippines

■ **Wedge-tailed Eagle**
Australia

E agles live on every continent on Earth except Antarctica, and everywhere eagles are found, people have traditionally viewed them as symbols of strength and dignity. The name "eagle" originally comes from the Latin word *aquilus*, which means "dark-colored." This word was probably used to describe a bird that most scholars agree was a golden eagle. The bird became *aquila* in Latin but was later called *egle* in 12th-century Europe—a word that referred to its sharply curved beak.

The 59 different species of eagle, in the order Falconiformes, are commonly divided into four major groups: sea eagles, serpent eagles, giant rainforest eagles, and booted eagles. Eleven species are classified as sea eagles. This group includes African fish eagles, Sanford's sea eagles, and bald eagles—the largest eagles in North America. Sea eagles are limited to habitats near rivers, lakes, and oceans. The Madagascar fish eagle has suffered greatly from habitat loss due to agriculture and urban development and is now critically endangered. The world's remaining 5,000 breeding pairs of Steller's sea eagles are found only along

Golden eagles are, like most other predatory birds, efficient hunters.

Golden eagles have been known to drop turtles onto rocks to break open their shells, enabling the birds to feast on turtle flesh.

Its occasional and musical whistling makes the short-toed serpent eagle one of the quietest eagles.

a narrow coastal strip around the Sea of Okhotsk and the Kamchatka Peninsula in Russia during the summer and at Kuril Lake in Japan in winter.

The 12 species of serpent eagle are found only in the tropical and subtropical lowland forests and plains of Africa, Asia, and southern Europe. This group includes short-toed eagles, black-chested eagles, and bateleurs—amazing birds whose moods are reflected in the changing color of their legs and faces, which can range from pink to dark red. The Madagascar serpent eagle is one of the most endangered birds of prey on Earth. Due to destruction of its rainforest habitat, this bird was last spotted in the wild in 1994.

There are only six species of giant rainforest eagle. As the name suggests, these eagles live in dense tropical rainforests around the world, including those of South America, Asia, and islands such as New Guinea and the Philippines. These are the world's largest eagles and include such species as Philippine eagles, harpy eagles, and Guiana crested eagles. Living deep in the rainforests of Guyana (once called British Guiana), a country in northern South America where 70 percent of the land

Twelve of Madagascar's 24 raptor species—including its serpent eagle, pictured—are found nowhere else on Earth.

remains untouched by humans, the Guiana crested eagle is so remote that it remains largely a mystery to scientists.

With 30 members, booted eagles (also called true eagles) make up the largest group. These eagles are named for the feathers that extend down their legs and onto their feet, resembling boots. The group includes

Like their eagle relatives, griffon vultures mate for life and hatch no more than two young at a time.

Australian wedge-tailed eagles, tawny eagles, martial eagles—the largest eagle species in Africa—and golden eagles, which are found around the world from the Arctic Circle to the equator. The golden eagle is the second-largest eagle in North America. Booted eagles also include hawk-eagles, which bear striking coloration in patterns such as stripes and speckles. The ornate hawk-eagle, a small eagle from Central and South America, has white and black stripes, and the changeable hawk-eagle, which **migrates** between India and Southeast Asia, has white and brown speckles or bars.

In general terms, eagles are birds, meaning they are **warm-blooded**, feathered, beaked animals that walk on two feet and lay eggs. More specifically, eagles are raptors, also known as birds of prey. As meat-eaters, they hunt for their food using powerful eyesight and capture prey with their strong, sharp talons and hooked beaks. The eagle's closest relatives are other raptors—hawks, harriers, buzzards, kites, and vultures. Eagles look most like vultures, except they have fully feathered heads.

An eagle's beak is made of keratin, the same material found in human fingernails, and it grows continuously.

After eating, eagles typically clean and sharpen their beaks by rubbing them on rough tree bark or rocks.

Normal use of the beak keeps it both sharp and worn down to an appropriate length. A hungry eagle is an efficient eater. Its hooked beak rips into prey, pulling flesh apart. Then, using the sharp edges of its beak like knives, the eagle slices off pieces of flesh from its prey's bones and swallows the meat whole.

Strong feet and sharp talons hold prey in place while the eagle dines. Eagles have three toes that point forward and one that points backward. The middle toe in front and the back toe are the shortest, but they have the longest talons. Like the beak, talons are also made of keratin and grow throughout an eagle's life. Clawing on the bones of prey and clutching tree branches and other perches keep eagle talons from growing too long.

To hunt, eagles rely on their strong vision. An eagle's eyes are located on the side of its skull, which lets the bird look outward and forward at the same time. This is called binocular vision, and it helps eagles judge distances precisely. The eye of an eagle has a nictitating (*NIK-tih-tayt-ing*) membrane (a see-through inner eyelid) that closes from front to back, wiping dust from the eyeball and shielding the sensitive **pupil** from direct sunlight.

A bald eagle's eyes are about the same size as a human's, but the eagle's eyesight is at least four times sharper than normal human eyesight.

Harpy eagles were named for the mythological monster with the head and body of a woman and the wings and claws of a bird.

Like their ancestors, modern birds have hollow bones, making them lightweight for flight. Female eagles are typically 10 to 30 percent larger than males, a characteristic that is uncommon in smaller bird species. The female Steller's sea eagle is the heaviest eagle in the world, weighing about 20 pounds (9.1 kg). Although it weighs less than the Steller's sea eagle, the Philippine eagle, at about 3.5 feet (1 m) tall, is the world's tallest. The harpy eagle has the largest wingspan—up to seven feet (2 m), and the world's lightest eagle, the booted eagle, has a wingspan of almost four feet (1.2 m) and weighs just over two pounds (1 kg).

Eagles have incredibly powerful wings. The wings of most eagles are long and wide, which enables the birds to glide for great distances without pumping their wings. Some species, such as the crested serpent eagle, have short wings, allowing these eagles to fly swiftly through forests while maneuvering around trees. The broad wings of eagles also help these birds lift themselves into the air while carrying heavy prey. The harpy eagle can carry its own weight and fly up to 50 miles (80.5 km) per hour through the South American rainforests.

Philippine eagles have broad wings and square tails that allow them to rise almost vertically between trees and vines.

An adult bald eagle has more than 7,000 feathers, yet its wings typically weigh less than 2 pounds (1 kg).

FANCY FLIERS

Most species of eagle can live up to 30 years in the wild or up to 50 years in captivity. Eagles reach maturity and are ready to mate at four to five years old. Most eagle species remain with a single mate for life, but if one dies, the other will find a new mate. To choose a mate, eagles perform courtship rituals that involve impressive aerial acrobatics, called flight displays. An eagle needs to know that its partner will be a good provider, and strong flight skills are an indication of an eagle's ability to capture prey for its offspring.

One type of flight display is the cartwheel. A pair of eagles flies high into the air—up to 10,000 feet (3,048 m)—locks talons, and then falls, spinning cartwheels in the air. The two break apart at the last moment and fly back up into the sky. In a stunning display called the roller coaster, one eagle flies high into the sky, folds its wings, and then plunges downward at a high speed. At the last moment, the eagle swoops upward to avoid hitting the ground.

While flight displays may serve to impress eagle mates, the behavior that secures their bond is nest building. Built

The bateleur is named for a French word meaning "tightrope walker," since it tilts its wingtips as it flies, looking like it is balancing.

in the tops of large trees or high on cliffs, eagle nests are called aeries. Both partners contribute sticks and branches to the nest, and most species will maintain a nest year round, making it larger and keeping it sturdy. A pair of eagles will normally reuse the same nest year after year—for 20 or 30 years.

Nests vary by eagle species and are anywhere from three to six feet (.9–1.8 m) wide. Bald eagles make some of the world's largest nests. The largest bald eagle nest ever recorded was found in Florida and measured 9.5 feet wide (2.9 m) by 20 feet (6 m) deep; it weighed 6,000 pounds (2,722 kg). Sometimes eagle nests grow so heavy that the branches on which they are built break under the weight, sending the nests crashing to the ground.

Most female eagles lay one to three eggs annually at a rate of one egg per day. Some species, including the golden eagle, can lay up to four eggs. The eggs are usually two to five inches (5–13 cm) long, depending on the species, and vary in color from dull white to pale blue or green to spotted brown. A group of eggs is called a clutch.

Like all birds' eggs, eagle eggs must be incubated, or kept warm, while the baby eagles are developing inside.

Researchers have found that if eagle eggshells are too thin, eaglets have a correspondingly lower survival rate.

Eagles shred meat with their sharp beaks before coaxing their young to take the food from their mouths.

Both parents participate in the task of incubation, taking turns at gently sitting in the nest with the eggs situated under the breast and wings. Depending on the species, eagles incubate their eggs from 30 to 60 days, after which time the baby eagles hatch.

A baby eagle is called an eaglet. Using its **egg tooth**, the eaglet chips through the hard shell of its egg. This may take between 12 and 48 hours. Most eaglets weigh less than six ounces (170 g) but can immediately eat meat that their mothers bring to them. Eaglets gain about a pound (0.5 kg) per week until they reach maturity, making eagles some of the fastest-growing birds in the world. Eaglets are born with light gray down and flesh-colored legs. The soft down grows darker and thicker over the first three weeks of an eagle's life, and its legs turn yellow.

Eaglets are weak at first and crawl around the nest on their knees, which are called shanks. By five weeks of age, they begin to walk and will shred the prey that both parents bring to them. Eaglets often fight over food, and in many cases, the first-hatched eaglet will kill its younger siblings in a practice called fratricide. This improves the remaining eaglet's chances of survival until it leaves the nest, as it will be the sole recipient of all food. In cold climates, where winters can be harsh and food scarce, a young eagle has a 50 percent chance of making it through its first year. In warmer climates, the chances are much better.

By the time an eaglet is 8 to 10 weeks old, feathers have replaced its down, and it can flap its wings, lifting itself off the nest floor. As it gains strength, an eaglet may leave the nest to explore its surroundings, but it will depend on its parents for food for another two to three weeks.

After eaglets hatch, one parent remains with them for the first two weeks of their lives.

The New Guinea harpy eagle is found only on the world's second-largest island, New Guinea, where it is the top predator.

When immature eagles molt, the replacement feathers come back in different colors.

Because eagles molt, or shed their feathers, intermittently in patches from head to tail, it takes about six months for all the feathers to be completely replaced.

At four or five months old, the young eagle is fully grown and ready to become independent. Because it has been so well fed, the offspring is actually heavier than its parents. But once it leaves the nest and begins hunting on its own, the young eagle will slim down to the same size as its parents. Depending on the species, a young eagle may not yet have adult **plumage**. For example, the white feathers on the sea eagle's body and the bald eagle's head remain black or brown until those birds are three or four years old.

As an apex predator (an animal that sits at the top of its **food chain**), the eagle helps maintain a healthy environment for all the living things in its habitat. Many kinds of eagles, including southeastern Europe's imperial eagle, help reduce the numbers of mice, rabbits, and other small animals that could damage their environments if left to overpopulate. Eagles also eat carrion, or the carcasses of dead animals. This aids in the natural cycle of decay and also helps reduce the spread of animal illnesses. In addition, serpent eagles such as the bateleur are among the few predators of venomous snakes, which benefits humans who live in areas where such creatures pose a threat.

Adult eagles have no natural enemies other than larger eagles. Humans have the biggest effect on eagle populations around the world. Destroying eagle habitat and shooting, trapping, and poisoning eagles are practices that have reduced the numbers of many eagle species—including the Japanese golden eagle, which has fewer than 650 individuals remaining in the wild—to the brink of **extinction**.

Africa's martial eagle will attack much larger prey—even young warthogs defended by their mother.

Danish 19th-century artist Bertel Thorvaldsen captured the story of Zeus and Ganymede in this marble sculpture.

KING OF BIRDS

No other bird in history has appeared in the art and traditions of as many cultures as the eagle. Artifacts dating from as long as 10,000 years ago show eagles being used to symbolize strength, honor, nobility, and fearlessness. The approximately 5,000-year-old Tomb of the Eagles, found in 1958 by a farmer on a Scottish island, reveals the importance of eagles to early humans. For about 800 years, the people of the island buried their dead in the tomb, and with the bodies they included eagles, most likely in the belief that the eagles would carry the dead to an afterlife. Thousands of human bones were uncovered, along with the skeletal remains of about 14 white-tailed sea eagles.

Eagles were given special status throughout the ancient world and were often connected to a people's gods and leaders. In ancient Greek **mythology**, the powerful god Zeus took the form of an eagle to carry away Ganymede, a sheepherder, who then became a beloved servant. In ancient Rome, Zeus was known as Jupiter, and the eagle was believed by the ancient Romans to be the bearer of Jupiter's thunderbolts. The golden eagle, native to

Ancient Babylonians believed a creature with the head of an eagle was sent by the god Ea to give them wisdom.

When the ancient Greeks marched to war, they would release an eagle to fly over the company of soldiers to rally their spirits.

Eagles can be found in art and architecture around the world, symbolizing power in ancient temples, palaces, and monasteries.

southern Europe, became the symbol of the Roman emperors, and images of eagles were sculpted in gold and worn on breastplates and shields as symbols of the Roman Empire as its armies marched across Europe and Asia from 27 B.C. to A.D. 476.

The eagle is a sacred symbol among virtually all **indigenous** peoples of the world, from North and South America to Africa and Asia. Because the eagle is considered the king or chief of all birds, eagle feathers are used as symbols of courage and power. Eagle images have appeared on masks, jewelry, costumes, and artwork in hundreds of cultures. Special dance costumes are worn

for traditional dances, and American Indians of the Creek and Cherokee tribes continue to perform an Eagle Dance today. This dance is used when greeting strangers and when celebrating victory in war or in competitive games.

Hundreds of years ago in North America, the Laxsgiik (*la-SKGEEK*), a clan of the Tsimshian (*CHIM-shee-un*) people of northwest British Columbia and southern Alaska, named themselves for the eagle, or *xsgiik* (*SKGEEK*) in the Tsimshian language. These people still claim the eagle as their clan's main symbol, and they have traditionally used eagle feathers and down in their sacred ceremonies. The Spirit Eagle's image is carved as a **totem** and worn as a

An eagle statue stands guard in the Cathedral of Reims, where French kings were crowned for 600 years.

costume, and clan members pray to the Spirit Eagle, whom they believe foretells the future and offers advice.

The symbolic importance of eagles to entire nations has persisted through the ages. Images of eagles appear on the **coats of arms** of dozens of countries around the world, from the European nation of Austria to the African country of Zambia, as they typically represent liberty and sovereignty. Like Austria, Germany's national animal is the black eagle, and an image of a black eagle has appeared on the country's coat of arms for at least 800 years. Napoleon I, who proclaimed himself emperor of France in 1804, based his new empire's symbol on the ancient Roman Empire's image of a golden eagle. Today, eagles appear on flags, military uniforms, coins, and currency around the world.

The United States' national symbol is the bald eagle. In America, eagles can been seen in the logos of the U.S. Postal Service, American Airlines, Harley Davidson Motorcycles, and in the American and National League branches of major league baseball. Eagles are the hallmarks of all four U.S. military divisions as well as the Canadian armed forces. The top level of Boy Scouts is the Eagle Scout; the 101st U.S. Army Airborne Division is known as the "Screaming Eagles"; and a U.S. military fighter jet, the F-15, is called the Eagle. When organizations want to send the message that they are the best, the eagle is the logo that conveys that statement.

Eagles have even been sent into space. In the summer of 1969, America's space agency, the National Aeronautics and Space Administration (NASA), sent the first men to the moon aboard Apollo 11. They landed in a lunar module named "Eagle." Astronaut Neil Armstrong, speaking to controllers at NASA's command center in

American patriot Benjamin Franklin called eagles "immoral" birds and wanted the turkey to be the national symbol.

The Philadelphia Eagles' mascot, Swoop, adopted in 1988, carries the team's flag across the field before a game.

Houston, Texas, uttered the first words from the moon: "Houston, Tranquility Base here. The 'Eagle' has landed." The eagle is so highly valued in human culture that even a constellation of stars in our Milky Way galaxy—Aquila the Eagle—and the Eagle Nebula, an area where stars are formed that is located 7,000 light years from Earth, were named for the king of birds.

Eagles also represent sports teams all around the world, from Arizona's Embry-Riddle Aeronautical University, whose competitive flight airplane team is the Golden Eagles, to the African nation of Nigeria, whose national soccer team is nicknamed the Super Eagles. In American minor-league hockey, the Colorado Eagles won the Central Hockey League's national championship in 2007, and in professional football, the National Football League's Philadelphia Eagles have appeared in the Super Bowl twice.

Two major rock bands are named for the world's most majestic birds. The Eagles, an American band from Los Angeles, formed in 1971 and was inducted into the Rock and Roll Hall of Fame in 1998. Eagle & Hawk, a Canadian First Nations rock group from Winnipeg,

Manitoba, has released eight CDs since forming in 1994 and has won numerous awards.

Because eagles are viewed as noble creatures, they do not often appear as comical characters. One exception was Sam the Eagle, a regular performer on the television series *The Muppet Show*, which ran from 1976 to 1981, as well as the Muppet films. Sam had a patriotic spirit and was presented as a dignified, if sometimes misguided, character. The name Sam (as in "Uncle Sam," the national personification of the U.S.) was also given to Sam the Olympic Eagle, the mascot of the 1984 Summer Olympics, which were held in Los Angeles.

The constellation Aquila the Eagle was known to the ancient Romans as Vultur volans, *or "flying vulture."*

Africa's crowned eagle flies above the treetops listening for monkeys before swooping down and snatching them.

FLYING HIGH

All birds **evolved** from hollow-boned reptiles that existed millions of years ago. A possible link between these two kinds of animals is the *Archaeopteryx*, a creature with feathered wings and reptilian teeth. It lived during the Late Jurassic Period, around 150 million years ago, and other birdlike creatures continued to evolve after it disappeared. Fossils indicate that the first raptors appeared about 50 million years ago. Scientists believe that a direct ancestor of the eagle lived in Africa about 2.5 million years ago and was the size of the crowned eagle that lives in African rainforests today.

As recently as 700 years ago, a species of giant eagle—the Haast's eagle, which weighed 33 pounds (15 kg) and had a wingspan of 10 feet (3 m)—lived in New Zealand. It hunted the moa, a flightless bird whose tallest species stood 10 feet (3 m) tall and weighed up to 500 pounds (227 kg). On the unique island of New Zealand, which had no **mammals**, more than 250 different bird species flourished. When humans discovered New Zealand in the 1200s, the island's natural balance was disrupted, and in less than

At one pound (0.5 kg), Australia's little eagle, the smallest eagle species, is a close relative of the extinct Haast's eagle—the largest species.

The ornate hawk-eagle raises its crest of feathers when it gets excited or startled.

Fewer than 600 Javan hawk-eagles still exist in their native Indonesian rainforest habitat; they are some of the rarest eagles on Earth.

100 years, more than 40 percent of the bird species—including Haast's eagles and moas—were wiped out.

While many eagle species are abundant today, some species, such as the Flores hawk-eagle, are dangerously close to extinction. Fewer than 100 pairs exist. Human activities are the greatest cause of widespread eagle deaths. Eagles suffer from electrocution on power lines, collisions with tall buildings and objects such as wind **turbines** and radio towers, and eating **contaminated** prey. Most eagles, though, are simply hunted or die out when their habitats are destroyed.

In America, despite being legally protected from hunting by the Bald Eagle Protection Act of 1940, bald eagles were hunted, trapped, and poisoned into the 1960s because farmers and ranchers considered them a **nuisance** animal. When they were further protected by the Endangered Species Act of 1973, bald eagle populations began to rebound. Today, more than 70,000 bald eagles exist in North America, and the species has been removed from the Endangered Species List.

An understanding of how humans influence eagles is vital to eagle conservation efforts. A series of studies

THE EAGLE OF FREEDOM

O, that Eagle of Freedom! when cloud upon cloud
Swathed the sky of my own native land with a shroud,
When lightnings gleamed fiercely, and thunderbolts rung,
How proud to the tempest those pinions were flung!
Though the wild blast of battle rushed fierce through the air
With darkness and dread, still the eagle was there;
Unquailing, still speeding, his swift flight was on,
Till rainbow of peace crowned the victory won.

O, that Eagle of Freedom! age dims not his eye,
He has seen earth's mortality spring, bloom, and die!
He has seen the strong nations rise, flourish, and fall,
He mocks at Time's changes, he triumphs o'er all;
He has seen our own land with forests o'erspread,
He sees it with sunshine and joy on its head;
And his presence will bless this his own chosen clime,
Till the Archangel's fiat is set upon time.

by Alfred B. Street (1811–1881)

Harpy eagles can spot objects as small as three-quarters of an inch (2 cm) from 600 feet (183 m) away.

conducted by the Santa Cruz Predatory Bird Research Group in California is designed to reveal the impact of wind turbines on eagle populations—specifically golden eagles, which live in the Diablo Mountains in west-central California. In Canada, the Rocky Mountain Eagle Research Foundation studies eagles that migrate along the "Eagle Highway," a route that thousands of golden and bald eagles follow as they migrate between Alaska and the southern U.S. across the Rocky Mountains of Alberta, Canada.

Such research has traditionally involved a process called banding. Birds are caught by various methods, including trapping and netting. Then the birds' legs are fitted with a metal or plastic bracelet, called a band, which is imprinted with a number or code. The bird is released, and then over a period of months or years, the bird is recaptured and identified by its band. This method of gathering data works well to count numbers of birds, but banding is not very useful in tracking migration and nesting patterns.

For projects such as those conducted on eagle migration, **satellite** transmitters provide a much better method of monitoring eagles. The transmitter is a

Global Positioning System (GPS) device that is small and lightweight enough to be carried on a bird's back. The weatherproof pack is situated between the eagle's wings. The transmitter inside the pack sends out a signal every 10 days, and a satellite picks up the signal and e-mails it to researchers. Transmitter batteries last for two years. The straps that hold the pack are designed to fall apart after that time, so the pack falls off the bird's back without any injury to the bird. Transmitters cost thousands of dollars, so researchers often try to retrieve them for reuse.

Transmitters are used on many eagle species, including golden and bald eagles in North America and harpy eagles in South America. In the case of harpy eagles, young **captive-reared** eagles may be fitted with a transmitter before being released into the wild. Researchers have found it nearly impossible to fit adult giant rainforest eagles—which are typically strong and fierce birds—with transmitters.

In South America, research on adult harpy eagles is done from a safe distance. The Harpy Eagle Conservation Program conducts research on the diet and nesting patterns of harpy eagles in order to understand the needs

The Verreaux's eagle, named for French naturalist Jules Verreaux, preys almost exclusively on the hyrax, a small African mammal.

The Philippine eagle is the only bird of prey that has blue eyes.

Conservation efforts are ongoing, but only 340 to 500 pairs of Philippine eagles, the national bird of the Philippines, still exist in the wild.

of this bird in relation to the human environment it shares. Researchers climb trees and position themselves on platforms near eagle nests, studying the animal in its natural habitat. The harpy eagle has feet the size of a man's hand, and its talons, measuring five inches (13 cm) in length—longer than a grizzly bear's claws—are the longest of any eagle. Researchers must wear helmets and armored clothing when observing harpy eagles, as a harpy eagle can kill a human with its beak and claws, and it can easily knock a person out of a tree.

The Eagle Conservation Alliance is a global organization dedicated to eagle research. One of the group's projects is taking place in the Southeast Asian country of Cambodia and involves the grey-headed fish eagle. Very little is known about this eagle, and its numbers are declining. What scientists have discovered is that these birds, while called "fish" eagles, actually eat more water snakes than fish. In Cambodia and other Southeast Asian countries, the harvesting of water snakes has increased to meet demands for snakeskin around the world. The decrease in water snakes has led to a decrease in eagle populations.

Wherever eagles are found, they must compete with humans for resources. In places all around the world, the logging industry cuts down trees that eagles need for nesting, and dams are built, flooding the forests and grasslands where eagles hunt. Research and education on the needs and habits of eagles is an important first step toward saving eagles from an uncertain future.

African fish eagles share their meals—consisting of fish or water birds such as flamingoes—with their mates.

ANIMAL TALE:
THE EAGLES' GIFTS

The native peoples of the Pacific Northwest believe in the power of animal spirits. The following myth about the integrity of eagles reveals the close ties that bind these native people to the eagle and cause them to share their resources willingly.

Long ago, there was a village next to a great river where the people fished for salmon. Eagles lived nearby and would follow the fishermen out onto the river.

"You are very skilled fishermen," the eagles would say to the fishermen. "Please share your catch with us. We are very hungry."

But the fishermen would never share their fish, and so the eagles would swoop down and steal the salmon out of the fishermen's boats.

The day came when the youngest boy in the village was old enough to go onto the river to fish. In his small canoe, he caught only three fish.

The eagles circled the young boy's boat and said to him, "Please share your catch with us. We are very hungry."

The boy knew the other fishermen would catch enough fish for the village, so he tossed his salmon into the air. The eagles snatched the salmon and flew away to eat in solitude.

The other fishermen saw what happened. They became very angry and told the boy to go home and never fish again. Suddenly, a great storm blew down from the mountains, and rain poured out of the sky. The fishermen's boats were tossed about by the raging river, and all the salmon they had caught fell overboard.

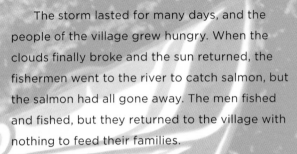

The storm lasted for many days, and the people of the village grew hungry. When the clouds finally broke and the sun returned, the fishermen went to the river to catch salmon, but the salmon had all gone away. The men fished and fished, but they returned to the village with nothing to feed their families.

The boy who had shared his salmon with the eagles went to the forest beside the river and called up into the treetops, "Eagles, because I shared with you when no one else would, please bring me something to eat."

The eagles agreed that the boy had been generous, and so they would repay him. They flew out to sea where the fish were plentiful. They carried many fish to the village and delivered them to the boy. The boy was so filled with happiness that he shared the fish with everyone in his village.

The eagles' hearts warmed at the sight of the happy villagers, so they flew out to sea and carried a fat seal back to the village. The people thanked the eagles. Next, the eagles carried a huge walrus to the village, and the people danced for the eagles. Finally, the eagles dragged an enormous whale to shore and presented it to the people, who celebrated for a week.

"We were wrong to be selfish," said the fishermen to the eagles. "There is plenty of food for all of us. We will be happy to share with you in the future."

When the salmon returned to the river, the fishermen fished every day. They shared their catch with the eagles, for there was plenty for everyone. That is why, to this day, the native peoples of the Pacific Northwest are happy to live in peace with the eagles that follow them as they fish.

GLOSSARY

captive-reared – raised in a place from which escape is not possible

coats of arms – the official symbols of a family, state, nation, or other group

contaminated – negatively affected by exposure to a polluting substance

egg tooth – a hard, toothlike tip of a young bird's beak or a young reptile's mouth, used only for breaking through its egg

evolved – gradually developed into a new form

extinction – the act or process of becoming extinct; coming to an end or dying out

food chain – a system in nature in which living things are dependent on each other for food

Global Positioning System – a system of satellites, computers, and other electronic devices that work together to determine the location of objects or living things that carry a trackable device

indigenous – originating in a particular region or country

mammals – warm-blooded animals that have a backbone and hair or fur, give birth to live young, and produce milk to feed their young

migrates – travels from one region or climate to another for feeding or breeding purposes

mythology – a collection of myths, or popular, traditional beliefs or stories that explain how something came to be or that are associated with a person or object

nuisance – something annoying or harmful to people or the land

plumage – the entire feathery covering of a bird

pupil – the dark, circular opening in the center of the eye through which light passes

satellite – a mechanical device launched into space; it may be designed to travel around Earth or toward other planets or the sun

totem – an object, animal, or plant respected as a symbol of a tribe and often used in ceremonies and rituals

turbines – machines that produce energy when wind or water spins through their blades, which are fitted on a wheel or rotor

warm-blooded – maintaining a relatively constant body temperature that is usually warmer than the surroundings

zoologist – a person who studies animals and their lives

SELECTED BIBLIOGRAPHY

American Eagle Foundation. "All About Eagles." http://www.eagles.org/all.html.

Dunne, Pete. *The Wind Masters: The Lives of North American Birds of Prey.* New York: Mariner Books, 2003.

Johnsgard, Paul A. *Hawks, Eagles, and Falcons of North America: Biology and Natural History.* Washington, D.C.: Smithsonian, 2001.

The Peregrine Fund. "Explore Raptors: Eagles."

http://www.peregrinefund.org/Explore_Raptors/eagles/eaglmain.html.

Weidensaul, Scott. *The Raptor Almanac: A Comprehensive Guide to Eagles, Hawks, Falcons, and Vultures.* Guilford, Conn.: Lyons Press, 2004.

Wyss, Hal H. *Eagles: A Portrait of the Animal World.* New York: New Line Books, 2006.

The golden eagle is the third largest bird of prey in North America, after the bald eagle and the California condor.

INDEX